Graystone College

Graystone College

RICHARD BARNESS

Lerner Publications Company
Minneapolis

Copyright © 1973 by Lerner Publications Company

All rights reserved. International copyright secured. Manufactured in the United States of America. Published simultaneously in Canada by J. M. Dent & Sons Ltd., Don Mills, Ontario.

International Standard Book Number: 0-8225-0753-6
Library of Congress Catalog Card Number: 72-7654

To Marilyn Granbeck, for inspiration

CHAPTER 1

I'll always remember that Thursday night in May when my pal Charlie and I walked into the neighborhood liquor store at closing time. The middle-aged man behind the counter had just opened the cash register when Charlie pointed a .25-caliber blue-steel automatic at him.

"Take the money, but don't hurt me," the man said, and he faced the wall.

I felt a shock of excitement race through my body as I helped Charlie scoop up the bills and the change, and then we were out of the door and running down the alley. Someone shouted behind us, but we kept running.

We were two blocks away when an unmarked police car pulled up behind us. I had the feeling that I was living a wild dream. But the two policemen who walked up to us with drawn guns were real, and the handcuffs that they snapped on my wrists were cold steel.

The feeling of excitement was gone. The roof of my mouth

was so dry that I couldn't swallow, and I felt sick in the pit of my stomach because I knew I was going to jail.

The next 48 hours were a nightmare. A burly detective advised me of my rights to have counsel before making a statement. I was then stripped of my clothes, searched, fingerprinted, photographed, and told that I could make one phone call. I wanted to call Mom and Dad, but I was too ashamed. I spent most of the first night pacing the floor of my narrow cell until I became so exhausted that I was finally able to sleep.

On my first morning in jail, I drank a cup of weak coffee and ate a stale roll for breakfast. An hour later, a young attorney talked to me for 15 minutes. He was a court-appointed lawyer who represented men who had no funds for their own defense. I learned that I could hire my own lawyer. But a lawyer would charge $2,500 or more for defending a robbery case. I had $3.20 to my name.

Shortly before noon, I was taken to a courtroom. My attorney told the judge that I was pleading not guilty. A preliminary hearing date was then fixed for my case, and bond was set at $10,000. I returned to my city jail cell knowing that I had to wait a week before I appeared before a judge again.

Shortly after noon, my lawyer and mother and father came to the jail to see me. Mom and Dad were kind and wanted to understand. But I knew that they were confused and ashamed. Their bravery couldn't hide it.

My lawyer advised me to plead guilty at the next hearing and I agreed. Dad gave me a $10 bill that I eventually spent on cigarettes and candy bars. The meals served at the jail were nothing like the meals Mom served at home.

The week dragged on until the day of my hearing. I was brought to court, and a stern-looking judge accepted my plea of guilty and transferred me to the county jail. I was then taken directly into a district courtroom where I pled guilty to aggravated robbery.

"A pre-sentence investigation will be made," the judge said.

The deputy sheriff who escorted me to the county jail told me that it usually took 60 days for a pre-sentence investigation. My home life, school record, social life, companions, and work record would be checked before the judge sentenced me.

Sixty days in the county jail cell seemed like a century. The days and nights passed very slowly. I had plenty of time to think—especially each night. I began to wish that I could close my eyes and force the nightmare away. I wanted to look around and see my room at home. But when I woke up each morning, I was in an 8-by-12 foot steel-walled cell that contained a thin mattress on a metal bed, one sheet, one blanket, no pillow, a sink, and a toilet.

I had plenty of time to think about that Thursday night when Charlie and I walked into the liquor store. A friend of ours had told us how easy it was to rob a store. He forgot to tell us how easy it is to get caught.

The 60-watt bulb in my cell didn't provide much light for reading. But I tried, even though reading a book or magazine couldn't make me forget where I was. I was buried in a building of concrete and steel, and a judge who didn't know me would soon decide if I would be placed on probation or if I would stay buried for years in the state prison.

Every night in the county jail was the same. The jailor brought in new prisoners at all hours. I listened to the jingle-jangle of his keys, and a peculiar feeling hit me each time I heard the steel door slamming shut. Even when I was asleep, I could hear that door slamming shut.

As I lay on my bunk at night, I sometimes remembered scenes from movies and TV shows about jails. But they didn't show enough. Cameras can't show the frustration and tension that a prisoner feels. Those feelings are a natural result of being penned up, but they are made more intense by the rules and restrictions. For example, my incoming and outgoing letters were censored by a jailor. I was permitted only two visits a week for one hour each.

I spent hours in that cell thinking about good food—a steak—a malted milk—french fried potatoes! I wondered what the grass looked like. I couldn't see it because the only windows in the cell block were 12 feet above the floor.

My 19th birthday would fall on the first day of September. I began to pray in earnest that I would celebrate it at home.

"Don't set your hopes high, kid," an older prisoner told me. "You'd better prepare yourself for a trip to the joint 'cause these judges feel a robber should learn the hard way."

When my girl friend, Kathy, and my mother visited me that day, I had to talk to them through a thick mesh screen in a steel door. I tried to act nonchalant and pretend that jail life wasn't too bad. But I kept remembering what the old prisoner had told me—I might be on my way to Graystone College, the state prison.

After the visit, the jailor gave me the clean shirt and the $5 that my mother had brought. I sat on my bunk and tried to read a magazine, but the words made no sense. I was very depressed.

For the first time in my life I realized that what once seemed important to me really meant nothing—the flashy sportscar I dreamed of owning, expensive clothes, a wallet crammed with money. I wanted to be important, in the wrong way. I thought I was really living when we parked out by the lake—sipping at vodka that burned my throat, popping speed pills, trying pot for kicks. And sitting in that jail cell, I also knew what

I wanted most of all—to be home again.

The car and the clothes I would have gladly exchanged, if I had them, for the privilege of being in the kitchen with Mom and Dad having a big slice of apple pie and a cold glass of milk. I wanted to wake up in the morning and smell the aromas of freshly brewed coffee and bacon and eggs. I wanted to be sunning myself on the back porch—free—free—free!

The big day finally arrived. I heard my name called: my lawyer had come to see me. He told me that we would go to court that afternoon. I showered and changed clothes, and my name was called again. This time I was escorted to court by two deputies. In the courtroom, my lawyer asked me to sit at a table in front of the judge. I asked him quietly if things looked good for probation. He smiled without enthusiasm and shrugged his shoulders. My hopes faded at that moment.

My lawyer began talking privately to the judge, and I dimly heard his voice droning on and on. I stared abstractedly at the ceiling, the walls of the courtroom—craving a cigarette to calm my nerves.

Kathy and my mother were among the spectators, but all I could see was a sea of faces. I didn't see Charlie because we were tried separately. I thought of the prisoners in the county jail who had told me to have my shoes shined, my hair neatly combed, my slacks pressed and looking sharp. I wondered then what difference it would make.

Finally, I was told to stand up and face the judge. The prosecutor began reading a statement about the crime. The judge's face was deeply creased and grim.

My lawyer then spoke so all could hear. He cited my good grades at school and reminded the judge that there had been no violence in connection with the robbery that Charlie and I had committed.

"And how do you plead to the charge of robbery?" the judge asked me.

"Guilty," I managed to say in a squeaky voice.

"You were advised of your rights to a jury trial? You received no inducements to plead guilty? You have had ample time to consult with your counsel?"

"Yes, sir."

The judge studied some papers that were in front of him. I felt my legs trembling, and the palms of my hands were wet. My throat was parched, and I could hardly breathe. I remembered that when I was a child, I used to pretend I was magic. I wished that I was magic in that courtroom, and that I could transport myself to some distant island where there were no county jails, courts, or judges.

"I don't like to sentence a young man to the state prison," said the judge. My hopes soared for a moment. Then he continued. "Robbery, however, is a serious crime, and citizens are often wounded or killed during the course of these crimes."

I stared up at the judge's face, looking for some sign of leniency, some sign of compassion. My heart was pounding, and my shirt was soaked with perspiration. His face was blank, and I strained to catch his last words.

"And, therefore, for the crime of aggravated robbery, I sentence you to the state penitentiary for a term not to exceed 20 years."

I heard the sentence clearly, but my mind refused to accept it. There was a dull ache in the pit of my stomach. My lawyer touched my arm, and we walked out of the courtroom with the two deputies. I searched the crowd in the corridor for my girl friend and my mother, but I couldn't see them.

"The best of luck to you," the attorney mumbled. "I tried my best, but there are so many robberies these days and the courts are getting tough." He walked away from me, into the crowd.

As the two deputies escorted me back to the county jail, they told me that I could appeal my case after I got to prison. I wasn't thinking of appeal at that moment—I was facing 20 years in prison. My head was pounding.

At the jail, I was permitted a final visit with Kathy and Mom. They were both crying, and all of us felt pretty miserable. In my cell, a prisoner brought a note from Charlie, who had been confined in a different section of the jail. He had received five years probation that morning.

I know that I sat there on my bunk in a daze for at least an hour. I wondered why Charlie got probation and why I got 20 years. It just didn't make sense to me. Was it because I had been arrested twice for skipping school? Or because I had had a half dozen jobs that I quit within a week?

A young car thief came into my cell. He wanted sympathy as much as I did at that point. He sat on my bunk and told me that he had just received 18 months in prison and his partner got only 90 days. Judges don't explain why they give one man 20 years and another man probation for the same crime. They don't have to explain.

The jailor came into the cell block and told three other men and me to get our belongings together. We were on our way.

I was taken to the jail office where I signed a receipt for my watch, lighter, and jacket. I had to wait 20 minutes for the other three men to be processed, but I didn't think that waiting was too important just then. I was facing a long, long wait.

The four of us were linked together with handcuffs. One prisoner asked if he could make a phone call. The deputy didn't answer him. We were led out to a waiting station wagon.

The prisoners made an attempt to act cheerful, kidding each other about the bracelets on their wrists. But I didn't join them. I couldn't make a joke of it.

I was seated next to a man going to prison for five years for a forged check. I lit a cigarette as the car moved out into the line of traffic, and I remember looking at the buildings, the people walking around, the cars that passed by. I was headed toward a different world behind 30-foot-high concrete walls. I probably smiled at the jokes my companions made, but I was thinking about Kathy, Mom and Dad, my friends. I had spent 60 long days in jail waiting to be sentenced, but after sentencing it seemed that the wheels of justice turned much faster. In less than two hours after my appearance in court, I was on my way—to Graystone College!

CHAPTER 2

The floor of the station wagon was littered with candy bar wrappers and cigarette butts. The driver and his companion, both deputy sheriffs, were protected from their passengers by a partition of heavy mesh wire. The back windows of the car were very thick. We were locked in securely, and there was virtually no chance of escape.

After we left the city, I spent the first 10 minutes of the 30-mile drive to prison just gazing out at the fields and woods. Then I took a careful look at my companions.

The man directly across from me was a tall, clean-looking fellow with black, wavy hair and a handsome face. He was about 25 years old. It was hard to believe that he was a criminal—he just didn't look like one. The man sitting next to him did look mean and tough. He was about 45 years old and had a scarred, sullen face. His hard-looking eyes caught mine and he smiled.

"How much time did you rack up, kid?"

I didn't want to talk to anyone. I just wanted to sit there and reflect upon the past and try to see a glimmer of hope in the future, but I didn't want the man to feel that I wasn't friendly.

"20 years," I replied, and then added, "for aggravated robbery."

He shrugged his wide shoulders. "You won't do much time 'cause you're a young guy and the parole board won't hit you too hard. I'm Hank Gowan. What's your name?"

"Jim Martin," I answered.

The other two men introduced themselves.

"Bert Spence," said the blonde man beside me.

"Boyd Sheldon," said the handsome man next to Gowan.

Gowan was the only man who seemed to be experienced, and he told us that it wasn't his first trip to prison.

"My third jolt for burglary," he announced casually. "I expect to be out in 14 months—at the worst, maybe two years." He lit a cigarette and appeared pleased that he had an audience. "You guys will feel much better in the joint 'cause it's easier to do time there than in a crummy county jail."

I thought at the time that Gowan was just making conversation, but I learned later that what he said was true. The food in the county jail was terrible, and there was no recreation there. The time dragged by. A man is kept occupied in a penitentiary.

"I'm a musician," Sheldon said. "Will I be able to practice music at all while I'm in prison? I got a three-year term for arson."

Gowan grinned at him. "Sure, kid, and it don't matter what you're in for. You can practice every night once you get out of orientation. In orientation, every new prisoner takes tests before he's assigned to a permanent job."

"I'm a baker," said Spence. "They let inmates bake?"

"Right on, boy, and they need good bakers," said Gowan. "You might land in the cordage factory for a couple of weeks, but you'll get in the bakery later."

"Cordage?" asked Spence.

"Yeah. They make rope now, but they used to make twine," Gowan answered.

He studied me for a few moments through a haze of cigarette smoke.

"What about you, Martin?"

"I can type," I said. "And I'd like to go to school if I can."

"You can later," he said, "and chances are you will wind up with a clerk's job 'cause they always need typists."

It struck me at the time that men who were on their way to prison would be more down-hearted, or sad, or self-pitying. But the group in the car and many others that I met while I was in the penitentiary had the same attitude. Each man adjusts in some way to the fact that he has lost his freedom. But for most, it is a temporary loss, and so they try to make the best of a bad situation. They wait, and do their time, and hope for release.

The July sun was hot. I thought about the summers I would miss at the cottage my folks owned by a lake in the northern part of the state. Then Gowan began to explain about the parole system, and I listened intently.

"We all see the parole board in four months," he explained. "That means we will see the November board. What the board decides depends on the length of your sentence, parole plans, attitude, and recommendations, if any. But it's not likely that any of you will be continued longer than two years. First offenders usually aren't unless they are serving time for a murder rap."

"The jailor told me I'd be able to get a work release," said Spence.

Gowan chuckled. "Man, those jailors and lawmen don't know anything about prison. It's really laughable. Some cop, or county attorney, or judge goes through a prison on a two-hour tour and becomes an expert on penitentiaries. What they don't know would fill volumes. For one thing, you're not eligible for a work release until you serve one-half of your continuation. That means that if you had your case continued for two years after the first time you saw the parole board, you would be eligible in one year—just eligible. There's no law that says they got to put you out on work release."

"How about us?" asked Sheldon. "Can we get out of prison on a work release?"

"Sure, but it's better to get a parole," Gowan answered. "Now you have to stay in the county jail when you get a work release. A man is better off getting a parole. If you're in jail, you leave at 6:00 in the morning, and you have to be back by 6:00 at night, and you sleep there. You are free during the work day, of course, but you also pay for board and room at the jail. That's usually $4.50 a day even though you don't eat your meals there. And who would want to eat his meals at the county jail?"

"What about cases like Jim's?" asked Spence. "Here is a guy who's not even 21 and the first time he's in a district court, he gets 20 years."

Gowan was smiling. "And here I am on my third trip to the joint and I got five years. Jim won't do as much time as a man with a long record, but sentences are still unfair. One judge who doesn't like forgers may give a man 10 years—another judge may sentence a man for aggravated robbery to a two-year term. Jim happened to draw a judge who is rough on robbers.

Y' never know. It's like that in every state."

The deputy who was driving called out, "Five more miles, men."

I stared out across the countryside, trying to catch a glimpse of the prison. No wall was visible. I could feel the muscles in my stomach tighten, and I took a deep breath to try to relax. The other deputy glanced at us over his shoulder; his face was bored-looking. The other men and I were just four more felons being transported to the penitentiary. I wondered if escorting men to a prison regularly had any effect on him. But I knew it was just a job—someone had to do the job.

"That's it, guys, straight ahead of us," Gowan said.

There was little to see at a distance of two miles, but I could make out high walls and guard towers and a huge water tower within the prison enclosure.

"Well, none of us got life so there is hope," said Sheldon in an effort to make light of the moment.

Gowan stretched out his legs and winked at me. I forced a half-smile and then realized that my hands were trembling. I didn't think I could survive two years or more in the state prison. The two months in the county jail cell had been very bad. I didn't think I could take any more. I couldn't swallow because my throat was as dry as sandpaper. I had chain-smoked cigarettes from the time we left the county jail.

The station wagon followed a curved road that dipped down into a valley. The other men and I could see the prison compound until the road leveled off. All that was visible then were the guard towers and the ominous-looking 30-foot-high concrete walls.

As the wagon approached the prison parking lot directly across from the administration building, I counted a total of six towers atop the prison walls. There was an armed guard in each tower—their high-powered rifles were slung across their shoulders.

"This is it," the deputy who was driving announced.

He parked the car, and his companion got out to open the back door. My right wrist was sore from the handcuff. Sheldon and I were the first two out of the car. As we walked across the street, it occurred to me that it wouldn't do me much good to break and run because my legs were so cramped from the ride. I don't think I could have run a city block.

At first sight, the prison buildings and front yard reminded me of a college campus. There were shrubs and flowers planted within a wide expanse of well-kept lawn.

"Hold it, Martin and Sheldon, at the top of the steps," the deputy ordered.

A woman and a small boy walked out of the front door. She was smiling until she saw the handcuffs on my wrist. Her smile faded fast.

I turned to get one last look at the outside world before entering the prison. The last thing I saw was a robin hopping on the lawn. Then all of us walked into the lobby of the administration building.

The marble floor was waxed and immaculate. We had to walk 30 feet to the first gate. Inside the gate, a guard pressed a control button that opened a second gate, and the three other prisoners and I and the two deputies went through it. The gate slammed shut behind us.

A prison guard searched us, and the deputy sheriffs removed their pistols and gave them to the guard. Then we passed through a third gate and entered a small room. We waited there while the court commitment papers were checked by a legal officer. When he was finished, we became official inmates of the prison.

The handcuffs were removed from our wrists, and we were

allowed to smoke for the first time inside of the walls. I saw several guards pass by. They wore grey shirts, black ties, and coats, slacks, and visored caps that were maroon colored.

Then the deputies returned with a guard.

"Good luck," the driver said, and he shook each man's hand. The other deputy did the same. The guard told us to wait.

"What's the delay?" Spence asked, laughing nervously.

"The papers have to be correct or we won't be accepted here," said Gowan.

"Maybe we'd all better say a fast prayer," Sheldon added.

Even I joined in the laughter that followed that remark.

I had barely lit another cigarette when a guard opened the door to the room. He called off our names from a clipboard he was holding. Moments later, the four of us went through a fourth and last gate into the rotunda of the prison. I learned later that it separated two cell blocks—A and B. The guard escorted us down a long corridor. A large sign indicated that we had arrived at the Deputy Warden's Office.

Several inmates wearing neat khaki uniforms passed us in the hallway and one of them called out to Gowan.

"How much you bring back this time?" he asked.

Gowan grinned. "Five years."

"Lucky boy, you could have done worse," said the inmate.

We entered the large office and then a smaller office. An inmate at a typewriter asked each of us a number of questions—names of brothers, sisters, close relatives, who we wanted on our visiting lists, extent of schooling, special skills, trade or military service, arrest records, and sentences.

The next step was to go downstairs below the Deputy Warden's Office. There another inmate fingerprinted us and took our photographs. Our prison numbers were attached to our shirt pockets. My number was 18903. Gowan said then that we would never forget that prison number as long as we lived.

Our clothes were taken, and we were each issued a faded green bathrobe. The inmate clerk asked me where I wanted my clothes sent—I gave my parents' address. The only items I could keep when I entered prison were my wallet, watch, cigarettes, lighter, glasses, belt, and shoes. The rest of my possessions were sent home.

"The money you fellows came in with will be credited to your account," the guard said. "From here we go to D block where you men will be kept in receiving cells until you have been examined by the prison physician and issued khaki clothing.

We marched up the steps and down another corridor to the cell hall that housed new arrivals. The guard in charge ordered an inmate to take us to a shower room. We had to remove our robes, and we were sprayed with disinfectant. Then we got under a shower.

"You guys will get three sets of uniforms, a dozen pairs of white socks, a towel, and a laundry bag with your number on it," said the inmate. "You toss in your laundry bag on Wednesday and you'll get it back Friday."

As we marched back to the guard's desk in the cell hall, the guard told us what our privileges were. A TV set was available in the recreation area—we could watch TV until 10:00 each evening. Library books and magazines would be distributed to those of us who wanted them.

"When can we hit the canteen, Sarg?" Gowan asked.

"Tuesday, Thursday, and Saturday are canteen days," the sergeant replied. "Men without funds will be given a loan of six dollars which will eventually be deducted from their wages after they are assigned to a job."

I wanted to ask a hundred questions, but I said nothing. I figured that I would learn all the rules from the men who had been in prison for a while. The guard escorted each of us to an empty cell. As each man entered his cell, the guard placed a name card on the door that listed the man's name and prison number.

"Okay, Martin, we'll put you in cell 101," the sergeant said.

I walked inside the cell and the door slammed shut behind me. I sat down on my bunk. There was a mattress on it, a blue blanket, two sheets, a pillow case, and a pillow. There was also a new drinking glass in a sealed paper bag on a shelf.

I stared at the green walls of my cell and, at that moment, I felt something like deep grief. It hit me hard. I was a prison inmate—no longer James Martin, citizen, but James Martin, 18903 . . . .

CHAPTER 3

By four o'clock that afternoon, I was settled in my 8-by-10-foot cell. I sat on my bunk, waiting for something new to happen. Then the guard brought me a set of earphones. There was a plug-in for them on the wall, and I could listen to any one of four radio stations. A metal slab bolted to the wall opposite my bunk was my table. I also had a straight-backed chair. There was a toilet, a sink, and a locker with a mirror on the door bolted to the back wall. A 60-watt bulb in the ceiling provided the only light in the cell.

"So this is to be my home for maybe more than two years," I thought. I studied a rule book that the guard had passed out to all of the new men. I learned that I could spend eight dollars, three times a week, at the canteen, if I had the funds. I could earn up to one dollar a day once I was assigned to work. Half of that would be saved until I left the institution, or until I had the sum of $150 in my savings account.

I learned that the wake-up bell would ring at 6:30 A.M.—that the light in my cell would be on all night if I didn't get on the chair or the toilet seat to unscrew the bulb. I could have a typewriter brought in or sent in by a visitor. I could also have a small TV set in my cell.

Spence was in the cell next to mine. He called out to me. "Anyone say when we eat around here?"

"Not yet," I replied.

I hadn't any appetite. Food seemed the least important worry at that moment. But it wasn't too long before an inmate pushing a food cart stopped at my cell.

"Get your cup ready for coffee," he said, handing me a tray of food through a slot in the steel door. "The guy behind me is serving java."

I put the tray on my bunk and stood at the door. The coffee man filled my cup and went on to the next cell. My first meal in prison was at least far better than the food served in the county jail. Gowan had told us that when men first come into prison it was common for them to put on a lot of weight.

The tray contained a hot pork sandwich, mashed potatoes, a salad, and a sugar doughnut for dessert. There was also a pat of butter and two slices of bread. In the county jail I had always been hungry, but I still couldn't eat much of my first meal in state prison.

The coffee man returned to give me a refill, and I took it. While I sat on my bunk sipping my coffee, the guard came by with a ball point pen, an envelope, and a large sheet of writing paper.

"You buy your own envelopes at the canteen. The postage is paid on them and you get eight for 72 cents. You have unlimited correspondence privileges and can write as many letters as you like. When you want a letter mailed, leave it on your bars. A guard will pick it up any time before 10:30

each night."

A single envelope was donated by the state. I decided to write to my parents and my girl friend and put both letters in an envelope addressed to my parents. They could forward her letter on. The coffee man returned with an armful of magazines. I picked out three of them and settled back against my pillow to read. But it was no use trying to concentrate on a magazine article. My brain was filled with so many questions about the future that I could only listen to my earphones and stare at the ceiling.

A guard came past my cell every hour on his rounds. He looked in on each man. The coffee man came back again with a library catalog and two cards. I found that one was used to requisition non-fiction books, the other, fiction. The books would be delivered each day.

I had a difficult time writing my first letter home. I wrote about all of the rules I had learned, and I told all of them to write soon. Then I ran out of things to say on paper.

The guard picked my letter up, and an hour later I discovered a new rule. I was told that there was no limit to money that could be sent to a prisoner, but it had to be sent via a money order—no personal checks or cash were accepted. Cash in prison is classified as contraband and having it is a solitary offense.

I decided to make a list of all the things I would write to my parents the next night. Then I heard a bell ring. Moments later a guard walked by.

"Bed time," he said.

I undressed and got into bed. I forgot that I had to turn my own light off so I hopped up on the toilet seat and unscrewed the bulb. The cell was not really dark like my room at home. A light on the wall outside the cell made it bright enough to read a book.

There were five tiers of cells, and there were 20 cells per tier. I was on the bottom tier, but I could hear the guard making his rounds every hour above me. His shoes squeaked as he walked past the cells. He flashed his light on each bunk as he passed. I was one of 100 men on one side of the cell hall. On the opposite side of the hall, there were 100 more cells.

I was still awake at midnight on that first night in prison. Another shift of guards came on duty at midnight. In the semi-darkness, I tossed and turned on the lumpy mattress.

I could hear a man above me snoring loudly, and now and then someone would call out in his sleep. I lay there thinking about what I should have done when Chuck suggested we rob a liquor store. If I had taken a dishwashing job for the summer, I would have earned $70 a week and been free to go to college in the fall. I wondered then if many other men spent their first nights in prison learning about hindsight. If only I hadn't done it . . . .

The radio was on all night, so I could have listened to it with my earphones if I had wanted to. But I knew that I had to get up at 6:30 A.M.

I began to do some mental arithmetic. I figured out the time off for good behavior I could earn on a 20-year term—not that I expected to serve the entire term. But if I did, I would have to serve 13 years, 7 months, and 18 days. If a prisoner had a bad record, he could wind up doing a flat 20 years.

If only I hadn't done it . . . .

It was after midnight when I finally drifted off in an uneasy sleep. It seemed like only minutes later that the shrill sound of the wake-up bell was clanging in my ears. I was wide awake. There is nothing more soul shattering than to wake up in a prison cell—starting a new day. I learned quickly what so many old-time convicts said about each new day in prison. "Each dawn you die . . . a little."

By the time I got out of bed, washed up, and made up my bunk, the food cart man was at my cell with a breakfast tray. There were cornflakes and pancakes on it, and the coffee man was right behind him. I settled for coffee that morning—two cups of java to start out my second day in the penitentiary.

The guard came around to each cell with a canteen slip and told us we could make out an order for supplies. They would be delivered by noon. I ordered a jar of instant coffee, candy bars, a razor and shave cream, envelopes, and a pen. When the guard picked up my order, he also told me to be ready to leave soon since all the new men were to be examined by the prison doctor that morning.

I felt fatigued when I lined up at the guard's desk with the other new men. I realized then that in prison I had to get my sleep at night, because when morning came, I had to go through my daily schedule. It didn't matter if I had slept eight hours or one.

The other new men and I marched over to the prison hospital with a guard. It took approximately two hours to get through all of the tests—physical exam, hearing and eye test, blood sample, teeth checked by a dentist, and finally, a chest X-ray.

We were all back in our cells by 11:00 A.M. I found three pairs of khaki pants with matching shirts and a dozen pairs of white socks on my bed. The guard came by to explain that we were all now orientation men. Since we had been examined by the doctor, we could attend movies that were shown in the prison auditorium.

"You new men dress in khaki now, and when the dinner bell rings at 11:45 A.M., you go to the dining room to eat your meals," the guard said.

The dining room was much larger than I had expected. It

was filled with tables at which four places had been set. I learned later that more than a thousand men could be fed at one time. There were two steam tables and I got in line in front of one of them with a tray. The first item on the steam table was boiled potatoes, then gravy, then meat that a cook served. A cook also served one pat of butter and the dessert. But I could help myself to as much as I wanted of potatoes, gravy, bread, salad, and vegetables.

Gowan, Spence, and Sheldon followed me to an empty table. There were two huge urns containing coffee and milk on a side board and a bin filled with clean cups. We also helped ourselves to milk and coffee.

The main item on the menu for my first meal in the dining room was pork chops. Gowan commented on the meals. "Coming out of those lousy county jails and eating here seems like the next thing to heaven at first," he said, and then he grinned. "The sorry part about a prison though is that they could feed us T-bone steaks every day and load us down with ice cream. But when the cell door slams shut each night, we are all hurting."

"Do we sit in the cell this afternoon?" Spence asked.

Gowan shook his head. "Nah, we'll be taking tests now for the next three hours, and then we'll attend some classes where the officials run down the rules and the programs available to a man in here. It's all part of what they call the orientation program."

When a man was finished eating his meal, he took his tray and silverware to a large wagon and deposited it there. Then he went back to his cell hall. I learned that cell halls A and B each had 512 cells, and that there were 200 in D hall where I had my cell. C hall was set up like D hall, but it was the maximum security wing. There was also room for 100 men at the farm colony outside the wall. As a new man with a 20-year sentence, I wouldn't have the chance to get out to the farm for a long time—a prisoner was a trustee when he was sent outside the walls to work.

When I got back to my cell after the noon meal, I found the items I had ordered from the canteen. The guard came around later and asked me to sign a receipt for the canteen order.

I listened to the news on the radio, and at 1:00 P.M., the work bell rang. Moments later, the other new men and I were taken out of our cells and escorted to the education department. There we were seated in a school room and given written tests for the next three hours. We took IQ tests and aptitude tests. The director of the department came up to my desk after I had completed my work.

"Understand you can type," he said.

"Yes, about 50 words a minute, once I get back to typing," I replied.

"Okay, Martin, I need a clerk up here and the job is yours if you want it."

"Thank you," I answered.

Gowan informed me that it was a good job as we walked back to the cell hall together.

"Beats working out in the twine shop," he said. "You might go out there tomorrow, but it won't take long before you are assigned to the clerk's job in the education department."

When I got back to my cell, the coffee man came around with more magazines. He looked 17, but I learned that he was actually 25 years old.

"I got twice your sentence," he said. "I'm doing 40 years for second degree murder." He stared at me thoughtfully for a few moments. "You know, I really blew my life away with pills, and I don't even remember shooting my girl friend when

I was high. Yeah, I blew my life away."

"And your girl friend's life," I thought.

I thought about the young coffee man later that night in my cell. It was impossible to judge a human being by his looks, even in prison. An old man who mopped the floors in the cell hall was doing a one-year term for hitting a neighbor with a hammer in a stupid argument about a dog. He was a kindly looking old man who didn't look violent at all.

Gowan gave us a rundown on some of the prisoners that night at the supper table. He pointed out various men as they filed out of the dining room after they had finished their meals.

"That blonde kid with the long hair is doing life for a double murder," he said, and he shrugged his shoulders. "And all those guys behind him are doing time for every type of crime imaginable—kidnapping, extortion, forgery, rape, and murder. I know it is rough for you new guys the first six months you're here, but you can always be thankful you're not doing time for a murder rap."

While listening to the evening newscast on the earphones, I remembered the faces of the prisoners I'd seen in the dining room. The criminals in the TV shows and movies were always men who looked like criminals—shifty-eyed, hard-faced, sneering and brutal. In prison I saw men who had committed terrible crimes of all types, and yet many of them looked like choir boys just out of church practice.

On my second night in prison, I realized what it meant to be alone—to spend hours in a cell with no one to talk to. The feeling of depression weighed on me like a cloak of wet cement.

CHAPTER 4

The moment when a man opens his eyes and sees the steel bars and the locked door is the most utterly depressing moment of his day. When I woke up in the morning I was invariably struck by the fact that I'd see the same bars and door for many more months or years.

On the morning of my third day in prison, I found myself thinking about the courtroom scene, hearing the judge sentence me to 20 years for robbery. I woke up feeling tired, and I knew that I had to try and get more sleep each night.

At home late at night, I would go down to the kitchen and have a glass of cold milk and a slice of apple pie, or I'd just sit out on the back porch steps for a while.

I was constantly reminded of the loss of my freedom by so many small things that a person takes for granted at home—no cold milk or slice of pie in the 8-by-10-foot cell at night—no back porch steps—no cool breeze to enjoy when the weather is hot and humid. The tiny cell becomes a man's own private oven.

I was washing my face moments after the wake-up bell rang that morning, when I saw two guards running past my cell. I heard the sound of a key meshing in a lock and a cell door being opened. A third guard came running by with a stretcher.

Men in the cells above me began shouting to their friends—an inmate had hung himself shortly before the wake-up bell rang. I sat on my bunk and could feel that the atmosphere was charged with tension. Again I heard the sound of shuffling feet and the guards came by with a stretcher covered with a blue blanket.

At breakfast Gowan filled us in on the details. "New guy—been here six months and served with divorce papers yesterday."

I sat at the table thinking about the blanket-covered stretcher, and my appetite disappeared. Did the prisoner have any children? A mother and father? When and why did the man decide to end his life? I learned later that he was only 29.

In my cell after breakfast, the guard came by with a clipboard in his hand. "Report to the deputy's office when the work bell rings, Martin," he said.

He stopped at Spence's and Sheldon's cell with the same message. The work bell in the morning rang at 7:50 A.M. When the other men and I reported to the office, a guard handed each of us a pass that read: "Shop G—Cordage."

We were told how to get out to the factory, and then we walked about a city block from our cell block to reach Shop G.

Shop G was on the first floor of a three-story factory. It was filled with machines that processed twine stock. The inmates working in the shop all wore blue overalls and light blue shirts. I saw that their clothes were covered with fine dust from the fibers that were running through the various machines.

We reported to a guard who sat on a stand that was elevated

six feet above the floor. He had to have a clear view of all the men in the shop. The noise was deafening, and the foreman who came up to us had to shout so that we could understand what he was saying. The guards wore maroon uniforms, and the foreman wore dark green shirts and slacks. The foreman supervised the shop, and the guard watched the workers.

"Martin, you help that man at the scale," the foreman shouted. "When a machine is filled with stock, you help pull the bale to the scale and weigh it."

Then an inmate asked us what size overalls and shirts we wore and gave each of us work clothes. I learned that men in the factory were not allowed to wear khaki uniforms during work hours.

The job I was assigned to wasn't really a hard job, but I didn't want to work there too long because it was too dusty and noisy. An inmate handed me a three-foot steel hook which I used to drag bales to the scale to be weighed. I learned that for an eight-hour day, my pay as an orientation man would be 20 cents a day, or one dollar for a five-day week. The men who were permanently assigned to the cordage factory made up to one dollar a day, but the average wages were 70 cents.

At 9:45 A.M., the machines were shut down. We then had a 15-minute coffee break and were also allowed to smoke. It was a relief to sit and talk without having to shout.

During the coffee break conversation, I noticed that most of the men, whether old timers or new men, usually talked about some aspect of their crime—what county they got sentenced in, the length of time they were serving, and when they hoped to be free. They discussed the parole board and reforms in the prison or the lack of them. But none talked about future crimes like the actors in scenes from movies about prisons. It is not likely that if two men did plan a crime in prison, they would discuss it in front of a lot of other men. At 10 o'clock we resumed work and didn't quit until 11:30 A.M.

We were allowed 15 minutes to wash up and be ready to go to the dining room at 11:45. Gowan came over to our table during the noon meal. "I'm back at my old job in the laundry," he said. "I doubt if you guys will be in the twine shop very long."

In the twine shop in the afternoon, there was a coffee break at 2:15, and we quit work at 3:30 and left for the cell hall at 4:00. I made a mental note to bring some instant coffee to work because each man made his own cup of coffee during the 15-minute break in the morning and afternoon.

After spending hours in the dusty and noisy shop, it was nice being out of doors as we walked back to the cell hall. I went to my cell and closed the door because the guards counted us as soon as we all got back. I was thrilled to see that there were two letters on my bunk. They were from my mother and Kathy. I know that I read both letters at least three times before I went to supper and three times when I returned to my cell.

Orientation men are permitted to watch TV or to play cards in the corridor of the cell hall until 10:00 each night. I also learned that we could take a shower every night. I watched TV for a while, took a shower, and went to my cell at 9:00 to write two letters. Kathy was coming that Sunday with my parents to visit me. Writing letters helps pass the time away and, for a short time, a man mentally transports himself miles from the prison when he writes to loved ones.

I slept soundly that night after spending a day in the factory, but I dreamed of the choking dust and the noise of the machines. There was no work on Saturday or Sunday.

I discovered that I could go back to bed after breakfast on

Saturday if I so desired, or watch TV, or lie on my bunk and read or write letters. In the summer months I could go out into the big yard. There were baseball and kitten ball games, horseshoe courts, and basketball and volleyball courts. Many of the men just found a spot on the grass and took off their shirts to absorb some sunshine. On Saturday night, modern films were shown in the auditorium. Most of the men attended the movies.

On Sunday morning there were Catholic services at 7:00 and Protestant services at 8:00. Breakfast was served late on Sundays and holidays—at 9:00. Dinner was at 3:00 P.M., and those were the only two meals of the day. We had three meals on all work days and Saturdays.

At 11:00 on Sunday, a guard came up to me with a pass. "Got a visitor, Martin," he said. "Walk up to the first gate and you'll receive a slip of paper from the guard. Then go to Cell Hall A where you check in with the guard there. He will let you into the visiting room."

The guard in Cell Hall A asked me to remove my watch and lighter. The cigarettes that I took into the visiting room I had to smoke or leave behind because none were allowed on me when I came out from the visit. It was part of the drug control program in the prison.

The visiting room was very large, and it looked like a hotel lobby. There were mohair chairs and sofas situated in groups around the huge room. My Dad and Mom and Kathy came through a door from the prison lobby. For the first 10 minutes we were hugging and kissing and when we finally sat down to visit, it was a few more minutes before we could think of anything to say. Then they began to ask a hundred questions. There were no recriminations. I was lucky to have a family that cared so much for me.

But we were ever conscious of the time limit. One hour whizzes by in the visiting room. It seemed like only a few minutes had passed, and then I had to kiss them goodbye and return to my cell. I learned, like all prisoners learn, that each visit produces the same heartbreak. A man must embrace his family and watch them walk out the door.

I had to stop at the guard's cubicle and remove all of my clothing for search. My watch and lighter were returned to me, and I walked back to my cell thinking of all of the things I had wanted to say but had forgotten during the visit.

The first Sunday night in my cell I lay on my bunk thinking about how pretty my girl friend looked that afternoon. I had to fight off a deep feeling of depression after that first visit. For a brief hour, my loved ones entered my life in prison and then, too quickly, they were gone. This was an excruciating part of my punishment—of losing my freedom. The more time I spent in prison, the more I came to realize what a waste my crime had been.

I looked forward to the following Sunday when my family would come again. My life would improve somewhat when I got my own typewriter and TV set from home. I remembered that I had read that prisons were called "country clubs" because inmates were allowed TV sets. I knew that those who protested most in the newspapers about coddling prisoners would never trade places with me. No matter what the privileges, it is still a sorry way to live.

That Sunday night at 8:00, I again saw two guards rush past my cell. A guard with a stretcher followed. The message was passed from cell to cell—a man had died from an overdose of drugs. He was 24 years old.

I learned later that in prison one could obtain pills and other drugs just as one could on the outside. But very few of the men took narcotics. The men who did so in prison had also used drugs before they arrived. The men who died from an overdose of drugs were likely to have died that way had they been free. But in prison, a death from an overdose was made a notable event by the news media.

I could hear the men above me discussing the young man's death for more than an hour. The sad part about an OD is that it is such a meaningless way to die. Some prisoners no doubt use drugs as a means of escape from the dreary routine of prison life—to battle the tension that builds up inside a man night after night in a small cell.

The inmate who poured coffee came to my cell that night with more magazines. He didn't have to be locked up until 11:00. "There will be a shakedown in the morning," he said in a low voice. "This kid who went out the hard way put a lot of heat on the joint. They will have guards swarming in these cells tomorrow when everyone's out at work. They go through all the cells and root up everything looking for dope."

"Why did he take so much?" I asked.

"Why do movie stars gulp down so much junk that they never wake up?" He shrugged his shoulders. "Got some guys in here who would gulp down a hundred pills if they had them. They don't seem to care about anything but getting that high feeling. The body can only take so much and then the lights go out."

"How did they find him?"

"The guard who passed by his cell noticed him lying in bed. He was snoring loud but he looked okay. The next time he made his rounds he saw that the kid hadn't moved an inch but his arms were dangling over the edge of his bunk. The guard became suspicious so he unlocked the door and found that the kid was dying. By the time they got the stretcher up there he was dead—just stopped breathing."

I lay awake until almost midnight that Sunday—thinking of my parents, my girl friend, the young man who had died. At 24 he had so much life ahead of him. I also wondered what would happen to me when I saw the parole board. I had served less than a week in prison and I didn't know how I could ever survive for one or two more years in that cell.

Lying there in the semi-darkness of my cell, it seemed incredible that men and women could serve many years in a penitentiary. One old man had been pointed out to me in the dining room. He had served 27 years for murder. I stared at him at the time and noticed that he was talking to himself. Some of the new men thought that the old lifer was comic—until they too spent some time in a cell. Most then realized that a man who could absorb 27 years of prison life was lucky that he was still alive and had some sanity left.

When I finally drifted off to sleep that night, I was hoping desperately that the official in the education department would get me a job in his office. I dreaded the thought of facing a Monday morning laboring in the dust and noise of the cordage factory.

CHAPTER 5

Monday morning was a lucky day. I didn't have to go to the cordage factory. A guard handed me a pass to the deputy's office. There I was told to report to the education department.

"Martin, you will appear before the classification and assignment committee within half an hour," said the director of education. "I have asked them to assign you as my clerk."

He asked me to type a page and was satisfied with my work. I wasn't too fast, but I knew that my typing would improve with a bit of practice. The job was a good one. I could wear my khaki shirt and pants at work, have my own desk and typewriter, and, best of all, I could drink coffee and smoke cigarettes any time. The fact that I could drink coffee and smoke when I wanted to meant a lot to me. Men who worked at jobs where smoking or drinking coffee was a violation of the rules had to sneak a smoke or a cup of coffee. They were subject to disciplinary action if they were caught.

At 10:00 I was called to the classification board room. A

guard ushered me into the room and I took a chair near a large table. Across from me were a number of prison officials who introduced themselves—the warden, the associate warden of custody, the associate warden of training and treatment, the captain of the guards, a clinical psychologist, and a Mr. Gray, my caseworker.

They asked me questions about my background, schooling, job training, and future plans. I told them that I hoped to take university courses by correspondence and get my degree in business administration when I was released from jail.

I was informed that the director of education wanted me to work as his clerk. They asked me if I was interested in the job. I said that I was. Then the members of the board assigned me to the education department.

I met Gowan in the hallway as I walked back to the cell block. I told him about the meeting.

"Good deal, kid," he said. "Be a few more privileges for you 'cause you'll be transferred out of D Hall now. You'll probably go to the A block. Got four TV sets over there and then you might get your own set from home so you'll be doing fine. The clerk job is a better go for you than factory work—see you later at dinner time."

The sergeant at the desk in D Hall told me to pack my belongings. I had to take my mattress, sheets, pillow, and blankets. He brought me a cart to move my things over to Cell Block A.

The officer in charge of the cell block assigned me to a cell on the third tier. I had to make three trips carrying my mattress and other belongings up the flights of stairs to the cell. In A Hall the cells were brightly painted. Mine was an apricot color, and the sink was new. While I was making up my bed, the inmate who mopped the floor on the third tier came past my cell.

"Want to buy a lamp shade and cord so you can have your lamp right over the head of your bed?" he asked. "Get you one for five packs of cigs."

He was back in a few minutes with a cord and lamp. I paid him the five packs and had a light right above my pillow. It was nice for reading and it saved me the trouble of standing on my toilet to turn off my light every night.

I had to report back to the education department after I was settled, and Mr. Wilson, the director, discussed my duties for half an hour. My pay of 20 cents a day was increased to one dollar a day for a five-day week. That meant I would have more money to spend at the canteen.

At the dinner table that noon I was happy to hear that Gowan, Spence, and Sheldon were also being transferred to A Hall. I didn't know anyone there and most men tended to buddy up with those they met in the county jail or those who came into prison on the same day with them.

That evening at 5:30, the men in A Hall were allowed to go downstairs in the corridor to watch TV, or to go to the gym or yard. I watched TV for a while. The benches in front of the TV sets had phone-jacks, and the men had to bring their earphones with them and plug them in to hear the programs.

Many of the men spent their free time playing cards, or ping-pong, or just walking around and talking with men they knew. There were 15 stalls with showers in the back of the cell hall, and I could take a shower any time until 8:30.

I got bored with television and went back to my cell after I took my shower. Writing two letters each night consumed an hour of time. I wrote about my new job, and I told my parents that I was gradually getting acquainted with prison life and looking forward to my university correspondence courses.

On my first night in A Hall, I went to bed shortly before 10:00. I lay on my bunk and listened to the newscast and then turned out my light. It was hot and humid in my cell and I couldn't sleep right away. I couldn't help but think about the November meeting of the parole board, even though my life in prison had improved. My job was satisfactory. I was being paid a dollar a day and I hadn't earned a penny in the county jail. A man can sit there for months awaiting trial or a court appearance and do nothing and earn nothing.

I couldn't complain about the food served in prison. And I could have a snack in my cell because I had money enough to buy goods at the canteen—cigarettes, instant coffee, candy bars, cookies, ice cream, canned meat, crackers, and jelly and jam.

But with all the recreation, the three meals a day, canteen privileges, and movies and TV, prison life was still punishment. I was awakened by a morning bell, went to work when a bell rang, went to lunch and dinner when a bell rang. I had to follow dozens of rules—some major, some minor and petty. I could be placed in solitary confinement for breaking the rules. I had to sleep in a small cell, and at night it was my world—for better or worse. If the weather was hot or humid, I suffered there . . . alone. I had committed a robbery and was doing 20 years . . . each night. I wanted to get out. I never again wanted to be in any trouble with the law, but I had no choice but to wait and see what the parole board members would decide about my case. They could continue my term for two years or three years. During the first four months in prison, I had no idea what the future held. I could make no definite plans.

I found that by keeping busy at my job each day, the hours passed quickly. In the evening I divided my time between television programs, taking my shower, and writing letters home. Then I read and listened to the radio until it was time to go to bed. A man in prison soon develops a routine that he follows faithfully, almost obsessively.

My friends were transferred to A Hall, and it meant a lot to me. I had someone to talk to and confide in. A man in jail without a friend is a sorry individual. And there were such men—those who had turned state's witness at trials, who had turned their pals in to the cops. And some men in prison were constantly seen talking to the guards. Those men were called rats—and most of them were exactly that.

I was like the majority of the men in the penitentiary. I wanted to do my time as easily as possible, without trouble, and then get home as soon as I could. I often read newspaper accounts about the prison and was amazed to see sensational stories about drugs and whisky. The stories were exaggerated—not that I was naive enough to believe that such things didn't exist. But they do in all jails, and reporters seemed too fond of writing stories about them that were amplified by gory details.

My friends and I went out into the big yard Saturday morning at 8:30. It promised to be a warm July day. We sat down on bleacher seats to watch a kitten ball game between prisoners and an outside team.

Later we walked around the yard. Other prisoners played horseshoes, lifted weights, or played basketball or tennis on the courts. I reached for my pack of cigarettes and took one out. Before I could light it, an old man walked up to me.

"Got an extra smoke, son?" he asked.

I gave him one, and he mumbled thanks and shuffled away.

Gowan grinned at me. "In here, kid, you got to learn that if you handed out cigarettes to everyone that asked, you would go through two packs a day."

There were two guard towers above the big yard. At least 700 men were in the yard, and the guards in the towers were always alert. There were two guards in each tower when the prisoners were in the yard, and both guards were armed with sub-machine guns.

"It's not likely a man could scale that 30-foot wall," I said to Gowan.

He shrugged his shoulders. "They have had no such escapes in the history of this prison, but in other prisons men have gone over the wall with homemade ladders, even though the guards were firing at them."

We were allowed to stay in the yard until 11:00, and then we went to our cells to be counted and to wait for the noon meal. The mailman came by my cell and tossed in two letters—one from my parents and one from my girlfriend. Their letters said that they planned to visit me that afternoon, so I shaved and put on a clean khaki uniform.

My name and number were called out over the public address system right after lunch. It was wonderful seeing my family again, and best of all, Saturday visits were an hour and a half long. Sunday visits were limited to an hour. My father brought my typewriter. But I had to wait until Monday to get it. It had to be inspected before it could be delivered to my cell. It seemed like only minutes later that the guard brought me the pass which meant that my visit was terminated. I kissed Kathy and Mom good-bye, shook Dad's hand, and watched them leave the room. I felt a pang of grief that lingered through the afternoon.

I was very lonesome that Saturday night. I found it impossible to read or to listen to the radio. I stared at the calendar on my wall and counted the days until the first week in November when I would see the parole board. To make matters worse, I knew the board would continue my case and I had no idea for how long. That was the hardest part about doing time—not knowing when the gates would swing open. It could be two or even three years after I saw the parole board.

I had signed up for correspondence courses in English and creative writing from the university. I knew that once I began my lessons, the time would go by more quickly in the cell. Gowan had begun to do leather-work—making wallets and handbags for women. They were sold at a counter in the lobby of the prison.

Seeing a movie in the prison auditorium was sometimes depressing for many of the prisoners, including me. We were reminded of so much we could not have. We lived in a world of men and khaki, a world without women, a world of rules and regulations, and our time was marked by the damned bells, bells, bells.

When I reported to work on Monday morning, my boss gave me a pass and told me to go to the Training and Treatment office. Mr. Gray, my caseworker, wanted to see me. I thought that Mr. Gray was a pleasant young man, but he apparently had little real power in securing release for the inmates he counseled. He could only make recommendations to the parole board.

"And Jim," he said, kindly, "too often my recommendations are not given any attention. I do prepare a resume of your case and background for the board. And before you see them in November, you will appear before the Inside Board here in the prison. This board will consist of several other prison officials and me. We will discuss your plans for the future, and then vote and decide how much continuation you should receive. We will report our recommendation to the parole board, but the board is not obliged to follow it."

"What do you think I will have to serve on this sentence?" I asked.

"Jim, I honestly don't know," he said.

"Well," I thought, "that makes two of us who don't know what to expect in November."

CHAPTER 6

I thought about my chances for parole most of the day, and in the evening in the cell hall I asked Gowan what he thought I would have to serve on my 20-year sentence.

"Who knows?" he said. You may see the board and get one year, and then again, if there has been a rash of robberies prior to your appearance, the members might hit you with a three-year continuation."

"Because a number of men outside commit robberies, a man in prison suffers the consequences?" I asked. "That doesn't seem fair."

Gowan smiled at me. "Look kid, you'd better prepare yourself. One time a cop was killed in a robbery a few days before the board met. Every man who went before that board got three years continuation, even a guy that had done seven hard ones."

"I'd better pray no one gets killed in a robbery the week I see the board," I said, with a weak smile.

Gowan moved closer to me and lowered his voice. "Jim, there may be some trouble tonight here in the cell hall. A bunch of guys are going to protest about the lousy conditions in the joint and we got to be alert in case the gun squad comes roaring in here blasting at anything that moves."

An hour later I saw no activity and so I went to the shower stalls. I was under a shower when I heard men shouting and cursing up by the front doors. I was drying myself with a towel when Gowan rushed up and yelled: "Get your pants on and head for your cell right now!"

I dropped the towel and pulled on my clothes. As I started up the back stairs to the third gallery, I heard gunfire. Before I reached my cell, I could smell the tear-gas fumes.

In less than 10 minutes all 500 men in the cell hall were coughing and rubbing their eyes. Tear gas is no joke; it hurts. I learned later that the guards dispelled the group of protestors with tear-gas shot from 12-gauge shotguns and with rifle bullets.

It was impossible to read or write a letter that night. I listened to the newscast on the radio. The announcer was telling the public that a small-scale riot had been put down at the state penitentiary.

The smell of the tear gas lingered all night, and when I woke up in the morning my eyes were still watering. There was no breakfast bell that day. A guard came by with a large pot of coffee; another followed him with a tray of toast and rolls. That was the morning meal.

There was no work detail that day nor for the following 10 days. I had plenty of time to read and write letters and listen to the radio. On the first afternoon that we were locked up, we were searched. Three guards told me to come out of my cell. They looked through my clothing and my cell thoroughly before I was allowed to go back inside.

For the next 10 days our meals consisted of sandwiches, cookies, coffee and, occasionally, milk. I listened to the newscasts and had to smile when I heard a reporter describing what had gone on in the prison. I was an inmate and I didn't know what had really happened!

When normal work schedules resumed, I learned that the men had complained about canteen prices being too high, about monotonous food, and about the lack of vocational programs.

There were 11 men wounded in the shooting, one man seriously, though he survived. All those who had been wounded had been running to safety in their cells. But the bullets bounced off the walls and struck them. No guards had been injured.

The prisoners had also complained about inconsistent sentences. I read later that a national poll revealed this as a widespread complaint in all states. A man with no past record could steal a roll of copper wire and receive a 10-year sentence. He would come to prison and be released by the parole board after four years. While doing his four years, he might see others sentenced to three years for stealing $25,000 with a gun.

No one would be able to convince that man that there was such a thing as justice. He would probably leave prison in a very bitter state of mind. And neither the judges nor the parole boards have to justify the actions they take in most cases.

I talked to my boss at the education department about having more vocational training in prison. "Jim, it would be wonderful to be able to train men in welding, or auto mechanics, or computers, or any number of other trades and skills, but there just isn't enough money. In every prison in the nation, at least 60 per cent or more of the inmates don't have a trade they can work at on the outside. When they leave prison, they are thoroughly punished but not very well equipped to start a new life in society."

"And are soon back in trouble," I added.

"Correct," he said. "If we continue to send men out who are bitter and unable to compete to earn a decent salary, we have failed the men and society. Mere punishment is not the answer and many of our citizens will have to accept the fact sooner or later."

I smiled at him. "You know, the guys refer to the joint as Graystone College—and a lot of the graduates are back for refresher courses."

"Well, it is a problem that few people seem interested in until there is a really bloody riot such as the one at Attica in New York," he said. "The penologists and the inmates know we need reforms, but too few others can accept the fact that our prison system is a waste and a failure."

He studied me silently for a few moments. "You know, Jim, you have a home to go to when you leave. But consider the prisoners who leave and have no one to give them help. The state gives them $100 to make a fresh start in a world where $100 is peanuts. We are trying to establish houses for men to live in on work release programs. We want the men to work at their jobs during the day and then return to the house at night. They wouldn't have to sleep in the county jail. Many citizens agree that it is better that a man be punished less and be given a job so that he can support himself and his family. It has to be better than sitting for years in a penitentiary."

"It should be no problem," I said. "Most prisoners would prefer to have a job and be gradually absorbed back into society."

"But there is a problem," he said. "The citizens will agree with correctional officials that half-way houses are an excellent idea, but they don't want to move inmates into their neighborhoods. These citizens have to make a choice. Do they want the convicts to serve so much time that they become bitter and angry and useless to society? Or do they want to train them to hold down decent paying jobs so that they can have a better chance of straightening out their lives and becoming useful citizens themselves."

That night in my cell, I thought about my situation a bit more clearly. I guess I was more fortunate than many of the other men. I did have a home to go to when I was released, and financial help if I needed it. And I didn't want to get into trouble again. I had had enough misery. I was fed up with prison life—the routine was getting to me. I was smoking more cigarettes—I was more nervous—time passed so slowly at times that I felt like screaming in my cell at night. Every day was the same. Nothing changed. Only my visitors made my life bearable.

August came and went, then September and October, and finally it was November. I was called before the Inside Board on the first day of November, a Monday. The only friendly face among the seven officials was Mr. Gray's.

"Do you intend to go to college when you are released?" the warden asked.

"Yes, sir, I want to get a degree in business administration."

Every board member asked a few questions and the meeting was terminated. I was scheduled to see the parole board within a week, and I wanted to know what the Inside Board had recommended. Mr. Gray met me in the hallway and stopped briefly to chat with me.

"Jim, I don't want you to set your hopes too high, but I can tell you this much. Half of the members recommended two years continuation. But the warden and the associate warden argued that since you were a first offender and since you wanted to attend college, a nine-month continuance was sufficient. The rest of the board agreed."

I walked on pink clouds for the rest of the day, but I couldn't forget that the recommendation was not conclusive. I didn't dare to even mention it to Kathy or my parents in letters. I had to wait to see the parole board.

For the next three days I could think of nothing but the pending meeting. I rehearsed the speech I would give. I knew that the board might ask questions that I was not prepared to answer at the hearing. I thought of Charlie, my partner in crime, who was on probation while I was in prison. I hoped that the board members would remember Charlie.

On Thursday morning I was called to the parole board room. Six men sat on chairs outside the room and were called in one by one. I had to wait for an hour before I was called. I smoked exactly 18 cigarettes. Each man before me went into the room for 10 or 15 minutes. Then they came out and several minutes later were recalled to learn their fates. I was quite nervous by the time the resident parole agent opened the door and said, "Okay, Martin."

I tried to appear calm, but suddenly my knees were weak, my heart was pounding, and my throat was as dry as sandpaper. I was told to sit at a long table. There were four men in business suits across from me. Only one of them was smiling.

"How are you today?" he asked.

I cleared my throat. "Fine."

The questions came fast. Some had nothing to do with my crime. Many things I had intended to say were forgotten, and suddenly a board member smiled and asked me to step outside.

"How did it look in there?" asked a man who was waiting.

I shrugged my shoulders. "I don't know. Honestly, I wish I knew."

Minutes ticked by and then my name was called again. I went back in.

"Jim, robbery is a very serious crime, and people have been killed in such crimes," one board member began. "But we feel that since this is your first felony conviction, and since your parole plans are very good, we will abide by the recommendation of the prison board and see you again next August."

I guess I mumbled my thanks and then stumbled out before they changed their minds. August . . . August . . . that was what had been recommended for me . . . nine months. I walked back to my desk in the education department and told my boss. He was genuinely pleased, but not as elated and dazed as I was for the rest of that day.

At 6:00 that night I was given a pass to go to the deputy's office to make one of the two phone calls that were allowed each month. My mother was so excited to hear that I would be coming home in August that she began to cry, and Dad had to talk to me. I told them to bring Kathy with them on Sunday and to let her know the good news at once.

Gowan, Spence, and Sheldon had also been before the board. Spence got six months, and the board had suggested a work release so it looked good for him. Sheldon also got six months, but Gowan had been continued for two years.

"Didn't expect much less," he said, seriously. "I have a record, but I will have only a little more than a year left to serve when I see them again, so I guess I'll apply for a work release next time up."

I went to my cell at 8:00 to write letters and sat staring at the typewriter keys for a long time. I was remembering what I should have said to the board, not that it mattered then.

I turned off my light that night at 10:00, but I couldn't sleep right away. I was already planning my first meal at home—a T-bone steak, a malted milk. And I could see myself gulping down a whole apple pie. It was fun to think of all the food I would eat when I got out of prison. I made myself a promise—at midnight on my first night at home I would sit out on the back porch and look at the stars. And there wouldn't be any bells ringing.

For the first time in months, I was able to sleep soundly that night.

CHAPTER 7

For the first few days after I appeared before the parole board, my case, along with others, was a general topic of discussion among my fellow prisoners. I was amazed at the number of men who knew how much continuation I had received. Men I had never met stopped in the cell hall corridor or at my desk in the education department to tell me that they had heard I got nine months. I asked Gowan about it at the supper table one evening.

"Sure, everyone's interested in what a man gets from the board," he said. "You've seen the list on the cell hall bulletin board. Your name and number is listed along with 89 other names for the month of November. The guys ask around about what you're doing time for. They learn that it's 20 years for robbery, and then they want to know what the board slapped you with. There are hundreds of inmates in here that you'll never know personally, but they're interested in what you got from the board. And they will also follow up on your next appearance in August to see if you did make parole."

"*If* I make parole?" I asked.

"Well, your chances are good. You're set up to go to college. It's your first felony conviction, and your partner got probation. You should make it in August, but a lot of cases don't make it the second time up nor even the third time."

I knew that Gowan wasn't kidding, and I started to worry again. "Why would the board give a second or third continuance in a case?"

He shrugged his shoulders. "Who knows? They might feel a guy's attitude is bad. They might not like his work report. Some official may see the board members and make a special request that a certain inmate stay a while longer. There could be a dozen other reasons, but you'll never find out about them if your parole is denied."

That night in my cell, I stared at the white slip of paper that I had taped to the wall opposite my bed—"continued nine months." I knew that many of the men taped up the board slip as a reminder of the month that they would again appear for a hearing. Those men who got a three-year continuation tossed their slips in the toilet. No one wants to be reminded that 36 months must pass before he gets another chance with the board.

Even though I'd received my nine-month continuation, I knew that I couldn't be sure of the future. So many things could happen. I could get involved in a fight without wanting to fight. A foreman or official might give me a poor mark on my work report. Old timers in the prison said: "Don't relax until you get your suit on, your $100 in your pocket, and you pass through the last gate. Then you know you are on your way."

My family and Kathy came to visit me on Sunday at noon. My parents were so happy about the break I had received that

I couldn't tell them that it was possible that I might get another continuation at the second hearing. They had brought me a small TV set for my cell. I told them that I'd be able to use it by Monday evening.

During that visit we planned for the day that I would be released. Dad was going to take the day off from work, and they would all be in the prison lobby to greet me when I walked through the last gate. My mother planned a family dinner to celebrate the occasion. Having them with me to make plans made the day seem very close. But all too soon, the hour was over, and they left, and I was an inmate once more.

From that time on, the only date that mattered to me was my next meeting with the board in the following August. During the winter months I sometimes went to the gym at night and sometimes went ice skating on Saturday and Sunday. But I spent most of my time in my cell after work. I had my correspondence studies to finish, and I had my own TV set to watch whenever I wanted to. So I kept very much to myself.

The seasons have little effect on a prisoner. The routine goes on whether it rains, snows, sleets, or turns balmy. As the August board date came closer, I found it more difficult to concentrate on my studies. I became more and more convinced that I could never again go through the routine, the drabness, the loneliness of prison life.

One night in early spring I was awakened from an uneasy sleep by a high, piercing scream. It jolted me upright in my bed. Someone had cracked up. He screamed and screamed, each time louder than before. Every man in the cell hall was awake. They shouted at the guards, demanding that they get the man out of the cell block. I could hear guards running on the tier above me—a cell door being unlocked. The echo of the prisoner's screams lingered long after he had been taken to a cell in the hospital.

It took a long time to get back to sleep. Everyone was very tense. I could hear the other men cursing in the darkness of their cells. I wondered if the guards would rather handle an insane man than a dead one. It was probably worse to check the cells late at night and see a man hanging from the bars, or on the floor with his wrists or throat slashed.

By July I began to lose weight. I lost my appetite and became very nervous as the August hearing approached. I couldn't forget that the board could continue my case even longer.

A week before the August board met, Mr. Gray called me to his office for a conference. He told me that my boss had recommended parole, and that he would allow me to make a phone call as soon as I came out of the board room.

The board met on a Wednesday, and I was more nervous than I had been nine months before. I felt quite weak-kneed when I was finally called into the board room. But the members were all smiling. I hoped that it was a good sign.

"Jim, before we discuss parole, do you honestly feel that you can make it outside?" the chairman asked.

"I know that I can," I answered.

Then they discussed my home life and my plans to enter college in September. I reminded them that I had a part-time job waiting for me at my uncle's garage.

Then I was told to step outside. When I was recalled to the room, the chairman handed me a slip of paper that read "parole granted." I turned to open the door, and a board member said, "Jim, don't let us down."

I know that I said something that I meant to be reassuring, but I don't remember what it was. I think I was close to tears.

I went directly to Mr. Gray's office and called my mother. This time she was calmer than I. After the phone call, I went to the tailor shop to select a suit from a large rack. I chose a blue suit, white shirt, black shoes, and a blue tie. I could have had a sports outfit, but I took the suit.

That night in the cell hall, my friends stopped by to wish me luck. I didn't know when I would be leaving, but as I watched television and saw the houses, automobiles, highways, and free people, I was jubilant. I knew that in a matter of hours I'd be out there among them—free as a bird!

The next day I was fingerprinted as I had been when I came into prison. My photograph was also taken, and the resident parole agent interviewed me.

"Your parole agent in the city is Bill Carlson. As soon as he confirms your plans with your parents and sends me word, you will go out," he said. I want you to call him as soon as you get settled at home. He will be expecting to hear from you."

I went back to my cell and packed all of my books, personal things, and my typewriter and waited for the pass that would send me out. Time passed more slowly that night than ever before in prison. Reading a book was impossible, TV bored me.

On Friday morning when I reported to work, my boss called me into his office. "I want to wish you good luck, Jim," he said, shaking my hand. "You are leaving at nine this morning. Your parents will be here to pick you up."

I tried to be polite and calm as I left his office, but as soon as I was out of the door I began to rush around. I cleaned out my desk as quickly as I could and went back to the cell hall. I shouted good-bye to as many of my friends as I could see. When I got to my cell, I unplugged my TV set and put it in a box. A friend helped me bring my three boxes of belongings to the officer's desk. All I needed then was the pass to the deputy's office where I would change clothes and be on my way.

When the call came, my friend and I again picked up my boxes and walked to the deputy's office. There I put on my shirt and suit. I had difficulty with the tie—it had been 15 months since I'd worn one. Moments later I was escorted up the hall to the inside gate by a guard. He carried one of my boxes for me. The resident parole agent met me there and together we passed through the second gate. I had to sit at a small desk and read the parole rules—keep reasonable hours, stay employed, notify the parole officer of a change of address, no drinking, no firearms for any reason. I was too excited to study the rules very thoroughly and was eager to be on my way.

Then the agent gave me an envelope with $100 in it, shook my hand, and nodded to the guard at the second gate. I walked through it and as I approached the last gate, I could see Kathy and my parents in the lobby.

I heard the guard at the control board wish me luck. I nodded my head and walked out through the gate to the lobby. Kathy was the first to rush up and embrace me. She was crying and so was my mother. I wanted to hurry and get out to Dad's car with my boxes. I remembered the old timers who had said, "You never know until you pass through the last gate and even then you'd better hurry before some official changes his mind."

The sun was shining as I walked out of the lobby door. I stood for a moment on the porch of the administration building. I looked across the well-kept lawns and trimmed hedges and then walked down the steps with my family. Dad's car was parked at the curb.

Dad and I put my boxes in the trunk. I opened the back car door and Kathy slid across the seat. I took one last look over my shoulder at the penitentiary before I got into the car beside her.

The administration building still looked like a college building, but now I knew what misery lay behind those lobby doors... beyond the marble floors that led to the gates. There was a world of iron cages there that housed 800 men. There were bells, rules, restrictions, prison numbers, lonely nights in a small cell. But it was behind me. As Dad drove away from the parking lot, I could say to myself with real feeling: *I'll never be back!*

ABOUT THE AUTHOR...

Richard Barness knows more than enough to write a book about prison life. He has been an inmate in a large midwestern penitentiary for all but two-and-a-half of the past 18 years. He was a very young man when he was arrested and convicted of armed robbery in 1955. Mr. Barness was sentenced then to serve from 10 years to life in prison.

Before this incident, Mr. Barness spent his early years in northern Minnesota. As a boy, he loved hunting, fishing, and raising hunting dogs. He maintained good grades in school and was active in the Boy Scouts throughout his youth.

Mr. Barness learned the craft of writing in prison. Since 1964 he has published more than 500 articles, short stories, and books. Much of his work, like *Graystone College,* has been written for young readers. When he is released, Mr. Barness hopes to become a rehabilitation counselor in a half-way house for ex-convicts.

1284